AF326602

Whispers of My Heart

Whispers of My Heart

Louise Kerwin

When your heart awakens to the joy
of life, love and romance

To all first, second and third loves,
we learn from each and continue to grow
Love will never be the same but will show us
the capacity our heart has to shine.

Dedication

To my daughters, Nicole, Tegan and Iszy and my son Jack thank you for all your support and encouragement on this journey

Love Notes

Wow, gorgeous Louise! Thank you for sharing... I absolutely loved the memories of the type of love you have evoked. The opening poem set the tone of the whole volume for me. In essence it's the love that matters – for self, for spirit, for my dog, for my children and grandchildren, and indeed for what I have lost.

You have a lovely way of setting a beautiful & dreamy scene... I particularly love the simplicity.

Let me rest my head upon your shoulder, Let me catch my breath
The warmth, the love, the safety I feel, Cannot be matched alone

CLAIRE STRONG NATUROPATH

I love whispers of my heart, Louise takes you on a wonderful reconnection with what it is to love deeply and, in the moment, through her amazing new poetry book, whispers of my heart. This poetry is a wonderful opportunity to connect with how you love and to ponder the exchange of true love and all its rainbows of emotion.

Thanks for sharing your beautiful heart, Louise, it was a delight.

LESLEY-ANN BERGSTROM SHAMANISM,
MEDITATION, CHANNELLING COACH & NATUROPATH

I feel like I want to just read a poem each day, and sit and be nourished and enchanted, this is a beautiful journey through love and part of me weaves along with the story going on between me and the love I would love to know that you have evoked.

Thank you

JULIE PARKER HERBALIST & LIFE COACH

A joy to read, my personal favourites are on pages 8 & 26, I am sure everyone will find their favourite in the is beautiful 1st edition by Louise

G Headley, Naturopath Coach & Mentor

When I heard about these poems, and then seeing the title of the collection, it called to me. I am not generally into poetry, but there was something about these ones that intrigued me enough to want to read them. And I have to say, that I have loved what I have read. The poems truly spoke the words, that if my heart could speak, would say. These poems are beautiful and reflect what I at times have felt and thought, and even more, surprisingly say those things that you haven't even put thought to. These poems are magical. Thank you for writing this lovely collection.

Carmen Alvarado

Where do I start? These poems blow me away. I feel like they are about new love, love that has been present forever, completely encompassing love and unimagined love. The intensity of the feelings you write about is palpable.

At first, I was looking for each poem to have a title, but as I read through the poems, I began to understand the thread running through the poems. Well, how they came across to me at least. It seems to me these poems relate to a love that is complete, new, unexpected but already known, all at the same time.

Christine Dashper Naturopath,
Aromatherapist, Reiki and meditation specialist

I set off on a journey
To find true love.

Never in a million years
Did I think it was to my own heart
So off I journeyed for over a year and a day
To find this love I crave.

To find peace within
And a love so profound
Not realising that to love oneself
Is the gift I was seeking.

Then one day I heard a song
Playing in my head.
I could hear my heart calling
It played for days and days.

I can still hear that tune inside my heart
She was awakening, she was waiting just for me
She had been waiting for a thousand years
and that brought me to my knees with tears in my eyes.

I finally got it. A love so profound
I cannot share my heart until I let her shine
With a love for myself so deep and strong
That I sing and dance with abandon.

So, thank you my heart, I will do you proud.
For now, I see my own true worth
So don't be afraid to love deeply, wildly, and fiercely
For I love you most of all.

What is love?

Sunbeams that dance on your skin

The wind that caresses your every move

Each step you take with courage towards your dreams

Is love really defined?

Or forever changing, becoming what is needed

What is wanted in the moment, a lifetime or beyond

What is love?

But the music that inspires me

And allows me to dance with carefree abandon

So, see with eyes of love

Love is not so easily defined

But is the magic within and what can be shared.

When I'm silent in the quiet of dawn my heart is listening

When I speak, listen carefully to how my heart beats

You will hear and feel that you are the giver of my life

Everything is beautiful with you inside of it.

When you are with me, I feel like I can achieve anything I set my mind to.

Your smile inspires me, your character amazes me, your beauty leaves me speechless.

You mean the world to me.

Let me rest my hand on your heart and hear what you say,

No words are required as volumes are spoken.

Trust grows and blossoms with each breath and is felt through the stars.

Feel my hand brush the hair from your eyes
And my thumbs touch the skin on your cheeks
I cup your face with my hands
I can hear your heartbeat from here
It's loud and powerful and matches my own
Sinking into your embrace is like the warmth of the sun
The song in my soul is getting louder each day
And it is a deafening I welcome
To sing that song with my heart for all to hear
Rest now my love
Another day is dawning
And our dance will start again

I want to hold your hand in mine
Fingers intertwined
I feel the warmth from your palms in mine
The excitement I feel as flutters in my chest
Feel like they will escape my clothes
The way we walk together, each step in
Time with the other
Over sand, grass, and gravel paths
Through nature our desires rise
Your hand in mine
I feel safe and protected

I want to see your eyes
As my lips dance across your skin
Each breath in time with yours.
I want to see your lips
Their softness in a smile.
I want to see your hands as they hold mine
The strength you have,
Balancing the gentleness in your heart
I want to see your eyes
With their sense of disbelief
I want to see your eyes
Lids, slightly closed
As I kiss each one lightly
I want to see your eyes
Shine with the love I hold
I want to see your eyes
When I wake with mornings first breath
I want to see your eyes
At how you look at me
I want to see your eyes
Twinkle with laughter
I want to see your eyes
With my reflection in them
To dance in the sun
The turning of the seasons
And in coolness of moonlight
I want to see your eyes
As I see your soul within
The laughter, the sadness and everything in between
I want to see your eyes, as my love shines through them

If not for you, I wouldn't know
What true love really meant.
I'd never feel this inner peace;
I could not be content.
If not for you, I'd never have
The pleasures of romance.
I'd miss the bliss, the craziness,
Of love's sweet, silly dance.
I have to feel your tender touch;
I have to hear your voice;
No other one could take your place;
You're it; I have no choice.
If not for you, I'd be adrift;
I don't know what I'd do;
I'd be searching for my other half,
Incomplete, if not for you.

If your love were an ocean,

I'd intently sip it so it would last a lifetime

If your love were the stars in the sky,

I'd patiently count them, so I know the number of years we'll
spend together.

Ever since I met you, I can't think what life would be without you,

Since the day I kissed those pink lips of yours, nothing tastes
more delicious.

I desire you more than the air I breathe,

My daydreams are filled with your smiles.

For a moment I've asked myself, who am I without you?

To truly love you and to be loved by you

I want to see you smile, the kind that lights up your face
The ones that make people stop and say I want what you have
I want to see you smile, the ones that make your eyes twinkle and
dance
The ones that other say, I wonder what is going on
I want to see you smile, the ones that fleet across your face
With memories of the day before
The ones that flush your face
The smiles that light your soul up for the whole world to see
And comment on how different you seem and want what you have
Is it a potion a powder a vitamin that makes you smile so
No not at all but love deep within the soul
So smile without realising, the twinkle in your eyes
And make others wonder and sigh
I want the love you have that makes you smile so

Life and the world without you is unimaginable.

You are the light in my gloomy world.

the happiness and joy in my life.

the peace and love that flows in my heart

my life and my world.........

You have taught me how to truly love

even when there was no reason to.

I am the luckiest one in the universe because

I am blessed with someone as amazing, beautiful, understanding,

and loving as you are.

My love will always flow and light your world.

Who would have thought?
Those six months ago
With long flowing hair
All shiny and clean
Draped over my pillow for all to see
Your hair so beautiful it's curls galore
Shining between my fingers as I draw you closer
To brush my lips against yours
And inhale your precious scent
My head is all giddy with the thought I can't describe

I feel my words are inadequate to express what I feel and say

They will barely touch the surface of the depth I hold inside

I am excited and scared at the same time by the emotions I feel

How do I express what I have never felt before?

What if they are not returned?

What if they are scorned?

What if I never have the privilege of them again?

The love I hold in my soul is deep and runs for many lifetimes.

Learning that to love myself if the biggest gift of all

For how can I share how I feel for you

When I cannot give to myself?

So, as I heal my broken heart and find a love so deep

I joyously share that love with you

The happiness I hold within.

Let it light up the darkness and shine to the world as a beacon

Of what love has become

The dreams that I never thought were possible

Now shine brightly on front of my face

The desires that dance in my body now have an escape

The love I have to share is for all to see

But only for you do I share my heart

The strength it gives, the peace it holds, there is no compare

I am so totally overwhelmed by the strength of how I feel

So happy to give this gift I never thought was real

So happy to see how my life is changing and only for the better

Oh, what is now possible with love at my side is so unimaginably
exciting

So, thank you my beautiful heart for opening up so

Allowing me to shine brightly to the world

Allowing me to find the someone who would understand the depth

And breadth of my soul

With no judgement or want to take it away

But to share for eternity and more.

To be part of my love and not be overwhelmed

To not run away but willingly hold my love I give freely

Without any motive to own

To know there is enough for them and the whole world to heal

Enough for me, enough for you, to grow and expand

To learn what it means to hold a love so dear

That will take lifetimes to express

Let me show you how I feel

Let me hold you until the end of time

Let me express the love I feel in all its different ways

In all it's different forms

A love so great there are no words

But the feelings you can feel

Let me rest my head upon your shoulder

Let me catch my breath

The warmth, the love, the safety I feel

Cannot be matched alone

I'll just rest a second for my head is weary

Let me rest a lifetime in the surrounds of your arms

The hopes and dreams that are found here

The love and passion I thought lost

To explore new beginnings

With truth and trust

Each feeling the way, with new sight

Of what the other needs

With care, love and desires never before seen.

Let me rest just for a moment my love

A moment to catch my breath

A moment to share my love with you

Each moment makes up a lifetime

Of thoughts and dreams

Of moments that are fleeting, fast

Those moments are made of all the memories that last

Love is like a delicate flower
One I'm scared of breaking
I want to hold on so tight and yet I have to loosen
For how can I love and not trust?
How can I feel and not see?
By allowing that inner part of me to permeate through all of me
Do I trust what I feel with an open heart knowing that it could be
broken?
Do I sing and dance with abandon?
And true love flows through my veins?
My trusting that all will work out
Allowing my body to speak
And I deeply listen
For she tells the world, not just how she feels and what she feels
Whether truth or lie
She is one I cannot hide from
No matter how I try to hide my true thoughts and feelings
The ones that scream, you lie!
My life for you is true
It's rich and complex
And scares me how deeply, boldly, my heart is true

Let me rest within your arms
Within your love profound
To share, to give and receive that warmth
From the depth and breadth of my love
Let me rest for a moment my love
Let me catch my breath
Life is not just all roses but it's
Thorns and roots as well
Let me rest a moment
Let me share our thoughts
Our dreams
Our life
Come rest a moment on my breast
Feel the warmth and movement of my heart
Surrounding and encircling
Caring just a part
Just for a moment my dear
Each moment of our lives
Together we share the little moments of each other
Come rest your head my love
As our whole life awaits
The sharing of our love
And allowing it to blossom

I have to trust in what I have never had

To feel those feelings again

So scared I will lose them and not be brave again

So, wish me luck

My true heart

Let this be real and true

Let my love be accepted and returned

Just as deeply and true

Your eyes twinkle as your lips dance across my skin
Your breath caresses, your touch excites
I feel as if the skin beneath your every touch is on fire.
The excitement, the chills and twitching it elicits.
The caresses with your vision excites my body so
Not in a million years did I expect your touch to feel like fire
That is burning my skin as well
The thoughts are just as strong as your touch
To make my body shiver
The depth of my love for you
Shows in every movement
From the way I hold my lips
To the twinkle of my eye
The graceful way I glide across the room
And the laughter that ripples so
It engulfs and surrounds every cell of me
It is infectious
So stand close to me and feel
What love so tender feels
As she dances across my skin
With each tender touch
The quiver of your lips
The sigh in your hips
As your love is felt within

It is hard to explain
But easy to see
How you affect my being,
With the grace of kind
I am so blessed
To feel this thing called love.
It doesn't just excite
Or release a giggle and sigh
But a feeling so deep within the soul
Not seen before.
A love's tender touch excites
Each breath dances across my skin
The shiver and twitch
The gasp
The catching of my breath
Can't be explained away,
Except for the love I hold so deep inside
Now comes out to play.
So hold on with your delicate touch
And a whisper in your ear
The warmth of my breath
The caress of my skin
The twinkle in my eye.
As I share my love with you
And the whole world to see
That you are mine and I am yours
No distance is too far apart.
There will always be a way my love
It's just not yet apparent
So hold my hand in yours

And breathe the air I breathe
And let me feel it dance across my skin
A love so deep
It expands with each breath I take,
A love that ripples across my skin,
The one I hold so dear.

The gentleness with your touch, the kindness in your soul
Flows equally fast
A moment is all it takes to change your perception
Of a loving touch, a kiss so gentle, and a fluttering if your heart
Ah what is fleeting across your face
A moment lost in time
Are you're aware of loves, lost look upon your eye
With each tilt of your head and flutter of an eye
Once what was, is now no more
Than a passing thought
For my skin does not lie of the memories that are held
The complexity of your scent the exquisiteness of your touch
Is enough to waken my soul
Just a thought away
When you stir the gentleness, I hear it in your breath
The slight moan that escapes your lips as you sigh
Of a love that has been lost
Is now just moments away
So do not be afraid my love
The feeling is oh so close
Once you have a taste of it
The thoughts the memories come rushing back
There is no holding them in the dark, but shining from within
A new love so bright
That I can't contain the love you hold within
You are safe my love, I hold you dear I will never let you falter
Your love in all its exquisiteness now shines throughout my space
I hold your love so close for each moment is so precious
You are safe my love
To express, to feel again
Within the surrounds of my arms

Love is not just the good stuff the flowers and the kisses

But love is there for the tears and tantrums too

For when you heart is hurting, and you know not what to do,

My love is there to comfort to hold and caress

To listen and hear

To help you understand

Love is not here to fix the broken but to hold you while you mend

Love is the glue that holds our hands; hand in hand,

The smiles, the caresses, the look in your eyes

The ones that say 1 have your back, for 1 love you so,

We can take on the world together, side by side.

Love is many things but best of all it's you, and how we

Support each other so

Love is not just flowers and chocolates

But a deep understanding of each other; our wants and our needs

Love is in everything we do, our thoughts and our wishes

But most of all my love, is that we are side by side

We are better together then we are as one

Working together to life's last breath

Understanding each other and still never knowing everything

But the love 1 hold for you, the love we hold together.

Love's first kiss and tender touch are craved by my being

Through your eyes your lips and hands

The deliciousness of skin tingling

The beauty in my vision

Breathing deeply, your scent upon my skin and on my pillow later

The thoughts and memories that dance across my vision like

Rewinding of an old movie camera

I sit and watch what was

And excitingly crave for later

Tomorrow is even more exciting, as our love grows deeper

The distance disappears with each tick if the clock

Until I see you here

My hands, my skin, my eyes are hungry for your touch

So, do not wait another moment

Stand before me quickly

I cannot contain my love for you

I no longer want to try

For my love is escaping every pore

Every cell for the world to see

I can no longer hold love close

As it is not stationary, but a moving force, with great momentum

That has me swept off my feet

Oh love, I cannot wait another second to share you with my world

To see your tender touch, your beauty   heart and soul

I hear the birds as dawn awakes

And as I gently reach for you

My love, with you, there's always a beautiful day to look forward to
With every rising of the sun,
My heart, my body, my soul and my mind craves for your
unconditional
Love and touch.
Your love is like the air I breathe and the blood
Pumping in my tender heart.
I always feel special whenever you're with me,
For as long as there's love's breath in me
I will never stop loving and cherishing you
Beloved

Loving you isn't the toughest thing to do
It is the easiest when I see the smile on your face
Your words are comforting to the soul
When my troubled mind hears you say you love me too.
My love for you is like the rising of the sun,
So effortlessly In the morning
And moon's light never fails shine her silvery glow at night
Loving you will remain my desire and my strength,
For this is the wisest decision as each second passes
I choose you, my love, as it is the thing, I can do better than
anyone else
To touch your skin and smell your smell
And rest between your arms
Your strength matches my softness
Your protection matches my passion
My love for you, matches yours for me
We are ready for the day to begin

Loves embraced me as it caught me from behind
Snuck up so quietly I never saw it coming
Whoever thought you would dance across my vision
With eyes wide open I see
The song being sung for all to see
Who would have ever thought
The music that I hear, is touched with the thoughts of you
Who would have ever thought
The richness of your skin I crave,
The magic that it plays across my skin
And stays for days and days
Who would have ever thought the memories can run so deep,
My eyelids close and you are there
Standing before me
My senses are excited as they remember your first touch
And the music in your laughter
I rest each night in your loving arms
And wake with you in mine
Who would have ever thought a simple smile
A glint in the eye, and a simple verse
Would be all it took to win my heart and hear me sigh
Thank you beloved

Your eyes cast upon me, linger on my body
Your lips follow where your eyes have just left off
Oh, my love how vulnerable I feel right now
I hold my heart for you to see,
What is resting below the surface
Be gentle my love, don't expect too much
As my heart has already given you
All the secrets that lay beneath
We are both so complex, yet so simple
In all our needs and wants
Lean a little closer my love
I have one last thing to share
It makes me nervous to share this gift
For It has be a long while
So my love I share with you all my wants and desires
There is no competition
But my love for you that never dies
And is seen as a twinkle across the skies
The gift of vulnerability that only we both can share
How precious to have but more to give
That is how much I value your loving touch,
Your thoughtfulness and love so true

There is so much to learn about how each other ticks
It will take a lifetime to listen
The depth of love we each hold inside
And how that is given expression
Through words, a sigh, a gentle loving whisper
A brush of skin beneath a fingertip
Or a caress that continues to deepen
Through actions that speak volumes
Where words don't even make it
Knowing what your heart is saying even before you do
The looks that fleet across your face, is like an open book
Please do not hide behind a library of unspoken words or looks.
Don't be afraid of what I can feel
As only my heart is listening
And my body is following behind
As we grow and learn what each other likes
This deepens our love between us
For now, and evermore for all to see
To set an example for those still to come
Of what a taste of love looks like
In just a little bite
I'm so grateful I get to have the whole delicious cake
And spend a lifetime eating a little at a time
So hold my hand, and feel my lips upon your skin
Stand on my right hand side
As life's love is just beginning

Is a dream but a dream
Or a thought taking flight
Of once was and can be again
Or a whole new beginning
Those first steps taken
That open my heart
To see what is possible
And not just a dream
When love hits you true
And is not a mistake.
The joy and the disbelief
Are all rolled into one
As how could I get so lucky
And find my right one
You are my perfect fit
The yang that balances my yin
The strength that balances my softness
The one who wants to play with me
And dance through life's journey

So walk with me, my love

And enjoy each new step

A time of discovery

Of learning and growing together

I wait for the day where my dream becomes real

Where I hold your hand in mine

And you hold mine in yours

It's not too far away my love

Just a moment in time

When I can share my love

My thoughts and touch with you,

And you pull me close in your arms.

It's just a whisper away my love

Just a breath or two

Till the moment I am yours

And you are mine

As we dance with life's abandon

For the rest of our days

Your tender touch upon my skin
Your kisses drive me wild
The usual calm I have
Is now a raging torrent
To touch you and hold you
For the rest of my life
The smile you put upon my lips
For the whole world to see
The happiness in my heart
Shines like a beacon
On a dark and stormy night
It's there to guide you home my love
To give you comfort and rest
As I lay in your arms and feel your strength
I realise I'm the one
The luckiest girl there ever was
To call you my love
So kiss me, and hold me
And don't let go
Until our final breath

Oh my, what a restless night
Of dreams I can't remember
Hold me in your arms
And scare those dreams away
Feel my face on your chest
Let me listen to the rhythm of your heart
As it gently calms my soul
Let me wake my love
With your arms around me
And your lips on my skin
To know that you are here
In my every thought
Brings comfort I never understood
So hold me my love, within your arms
For the rest of time
As I share my love with you

My heart is soft and tender as a babe
Learning how to walk,
Having to trust in each step she takes
Is exciting and filled with wonder.
There are times when she falls and stumbles
Not knowing what to do
Reaching out a hand to brace
It's ok, it was just a wobble
So much new ground to cover
Be brave my loving heart
The love you hold is true
As I sit in the darkness
Awakened with a start
Am I dreaming? Is this real?
As I try to calm my heart
It's dark outside, quiet and still
Yet I hear my heart beating as loud as a drum
It's ok, my gentle heart
It was only a dream
It was not true
Rest my heart in a love so beautiful
So soft and caring
Rest
Another day is dawning
Another day to see the wonder in each breath
To see what love holds dear
A precious gift that is given
To one who holds it near
This gift is given freely
As she holds you close by.

My love is true and exciting
I want to share you with my world
I want to know everything about you
To learn, to love and grow
To say, look here he's my man
Standing by my side so tall and strong
But you should see his heart
So beautiful inside
As I rest my hand in yours
You asked if I believed in fate
And I said I do
A love so profound
A trust that builds
A friendship that grows
Through life's ups and downs.
To know you have my back
As I have yours.

I feel loved

I am in love

My heart opens

You are my passion

My loving delight

You are my healing

My bliss

And my Divine inspiration

With passionate gratitude and a hunger for you

The miraculous medicine of love

Let me feed our vitality

With love and grace as it is

Divinely given

Love blossoms when I'm with you

The warmth that I feel fills my heart

When I look into your eyes, I see the past hurt

That my gaze helps you to erase.

I feel your love emanating from every pore

The distance between us is so far,

And yet not at all

The depth of our love grows each day,

And continues to strengthen

I can't wait till I can be by your side

To hold you, love you and be loved by you

Till the end of time

Your words are music bring tears of joy to my eyes,

The depth of your love I was unaware

Your love so pure and true

You are the only one for me and

I am the only one for you.

Hand in hand

Side by side

We walk the path called life

With each step we take together

Our love grows stronger that can't be denied

We face the world together as we have each other's backs

You are my drummer and I am your drum

And the music we play is our own song

Your touch dances across my skin
Sending tingles along my spine
Your words softly spoken is music to my ears
With each breath I take I want to call your name
I want to say I love you
For all the world to hear
I want to see the seasons change
With your hand in mine
To see the autumn colours and the leaves paint the sky
To feel the cold of winter's touch so I can
Snuggle into your chest
And springs delicate blossoms that we walk beneath
As they shower upon us.
The summer sun shines brightly though she can burn
But a swim in cool waters with you by my side
Is filled with summer's laughter.
So walk with me my love, into the bountiful harvest
And see the fruits we sowed
Our love keeps on growing and deepening
With the turning of the sun
We sit and watch the sunsets and the moon rises
Hand in hand with my head on your shoulder
As our love grows and we get older
The stories we have to tell of our life together
Will fill our books
Chapter after chapter
For all to read and say I want the love they shared
And feel the warmth inside
Let's walk this journey together
Hand in hand and watch the seasons change
My love for you deepens as yours grows inside .

Not a moment goes by that your
face doesn't dance across my vision
Your name permeates my lips with
each breath I take
The sound of your voice whispers
on your tongue for my ears to hear
My hand reaches for yours and I
feel our fingers entwined
You pull me towards you and hold
me tight
I look up into your eyes and
Breathe
Never let me go
As much as you protect me
I want to protect you as well
You're more than what I dreamt of
and you've given me so much
happiness, peace and love.
No words will be
enough to express how
much I love you.
I love you so much is all I can
come up with because
my love for you is
verbally indescribable.
Thanks for being the
best thing that has ever
happened to me and
thanks for everything
you can imagine.
I love you beyond words.

You opened my eyes to many possibilities
Within the uncertainties of life.
With you, there's always a reason
To look forward to a better tomorrow.
With you, the future is bright and beautiful,
And I'm blessed to have you.
You're the sunshine in my life
And the light in my gloomy world, beloved

When I look into your eyes, I see the wonder there

How could I get so lucky?

There are days I see the pain as it flutters across your face

There is a calmness that you hide behind

Afraid to let anyone in

There was a crack just a tiny one as I slipped inside

I was just a whisper caressing your thoughts

And as each day passed it got louder and louder .

I'm here my love just for you, don't be afraid any longer.

The love we share strengthens each other

There is no task, issue or problem

That we cannot overcome

For our love that has come together

Is a force second to none.

The day you walked into my life
I was taken by surprise
A friendship grew, and a love unexpected
Which made my head spin
The moments I get to share with you
Brighten my day, you put a smile upon my lips
And my eyes sparkle like diamonds.
Everyone around me says there is a glow
That is your doing, my love
The warmth and the love you give to me
Filled me up inside
I walk with a dance in each step
As I imagine walking side by side.
So thank you my love, for the gift you gave
That I hold so tenderly

As I surrender into life's ease and flow

I come upon rest in your arms

As my head falls back upon your shoulder

A calmness overflows

You hold me gently but firmly

So I feel protected, and safe

That all life may throw at us I can rest within your arms

I can rest my weary head and move with life's grace

Knowing you have my back

My heart and soul wrapped in your arms so safe

So thank you, for holding me

Protecting me and loving me in life's grace

The sigh that escapes my lips

The sigh of trust so profound

Knowing I am safe in the surrounding of your arms

Upon your tender lips, life's colour flows
From beautiful reds to cool icy blue
From your heart shines a yellow so pure
A light as bright as the sun
Every time I stand next to you the light shines upon our souls
And fills it to the brim
The colours that swirl and move
Are distinctive and pure
No muddiness here
I wish the world could see
The colours you shine so bright
The colours just for me as love holds me tight
The colours we make together
As our souls entwine
Are filled with richness, and hues never seen before
I wish the world could see and appreciate the wonder
Of what our life together looks like in a world of colour
I feel your gaze as it dances over my skin
With hands on fire as they follow after
With a gasp and a sigh as the air slips past my lips
Your arms encase me and pull me closer
You whisper my name
And another sigh escapes
The thrill of your hands as they explore
Every curve every line every softness
With great care
Your lips dance across my skin
Leaving trails of shivers and fire
I try to hold my breath
But your name escapes my lips

Oh my love

Pull me closer

The glistening of our skin

There are no words

Only sensations

Of what has just begun

The excitement that flows as a breath dance across our skin

How can I explain the connection between us
When I don't understand it myself
The thoughts, feeling and sensations I feel
I'm sure you must feel as well
There are miles and miles between us
But I can feel your lips as they brush across my skin
Oh love how is this possible
To be so connected to feel your every shiver
As if it was my own
I am grateful and blessed that you can feel me also
It won't be much longer my love
Till I can hold you close, as your arms enfold around me
Under the moon's soft light
That day is almost upon us, just another breath or two
I can wait if it means loving you with all my heart
Till the end of time

I can't take my hands off you
When our lips meet and I can taste you
There is nothing else
Walk with me
Hold me
Be by my side
Step by step
Kiss me with your heart and mind
With your hands in the small of my back

When I look outside into the sky above
The twinkling of the stars bring such a delight
Knowing I am part of them,
A peace that is in my soul,
My love for you deepens and continues to grow.
The stars where you are, are different to mine
Seen from another hemisphere
They still sparkle and shine so brightly and show
We are connected through space and time .
Just look to the sky and you will see
My love for you shines as bright
As the sun in a distant galaxy
In a day, a week, a month or a blink of an eye
Our sky will be the same
So when I look up, and see the twinkling of that star
It's our love shining brightly
I know you see the same as me.
I will buy that star and call it ours for the world to see
Our love twinkles like a cut diamond in a sea of quartz
A new day is beginning; the sun is starting to rise
The light from our star shines just as brightly
But pales in our sun.
So love when you look upon the night sky
No matter where you are,
Find our star and know our true love
Shines for you to see.

Winter's breeze is cool and sharp as it dances round my head

Tugging at my hair and turning my cheeks a pinky red

You wrap your arms around me to try and keep me warm.

You hold my hands in yours and with a breath, try to warm them

I feel the warmth of your breath on my skin

Is like a fire in my heart that warms and soothes my soul.

The day is near where the seasons change

And the blossoms begin to shine,

The wind is now a gentle breeze dancing across time

My hand you hold still so tight, and our fingers interlaced

You pull me in and whisper in my ear,

I feel your breath on my face and my name upon your lips,

I still get excited hearing the way you say my name,

Even after all these years

I feel the fluttering of my heart as she beats in time with yours

I hold your hand as much as you hold mine

I stare with wonder as I look into your eyes

The love we share is so deep and true

We have weathered all life has given us

And it has strengthened us so

Our love keeps on growing with each breath we take

May the light of the universe continue to whisper to you my love
Showing you what you have accomplished
And what is still to come.
These little whispers of love that
Permeate your soul and fill your heart with my love for you
Feel the warmth as you lay asleep each night
And know that I am with you,
Beside you, hand in hand
The whispers of your voice calms, grounds and strengthens me
To take on life to see what is before us
Side by side
These whispers run around me and light up my soul
To match the love you provide with each day's breath
To be cherished and loved by you is all I need,
To hear you whisper my name on your lips
As you hear yours on mine.

With you there is a peace that overflows through me
A peace that I never knew existed
A balance that completes me
A love that grows inside
The feelings I feel and the emotions that swirl
Throughout my body and mind
To be loved and cherished by you is food for my soul
If I can give you as much as I receive from you
There will never be a hunger that is not fed
A soul that is filled to overflowing
A love that grows day by day
I am here for you when days are dark and when they shine brightly
I am here when you don't think you need me
But you do
I wrap my arms and heart around you
And say I do
My love grows with each breath we take for together we are
stronger
Than if we are apart

They say the time before dawn is the hardest
Before the sun comes up and shines her light over you
The birds are starting to wake
And the restlessness in me is starting to settle
Being apart from you is so hard, that I don't know what to do
I try to keep busy but thoughts of you are everywhere my mind
settles,
The thought of how your lips feel on mine, as they brush against
my skin
How your hands so warm and comforting hold me tight in your
arms
Your touch as it glides over my body and excites every inch
Knowing I'm loved and safe within your touch and the embrace
of your arms.
How I can get lost looking into your eyes as my love overflows,
I see your love, you are the one, I want to spend the rest of my
life with
Walk by your side, to hold your hand in mine
To watch you grow and shine, to say look there's my love
So handsome and kind, I truly am the luckiest one
For the rest of our lives

To rest in your embrace, to feel safe and warm

To feel my heart expanding as she pops out of my chest

My love for you grows each day with each passing breath

The birds sing your song to me

Each and every day

Even when it's dark right before dawn I hear your love all
around me

With each and every song

There are days I didn't think my love could grow any more

But you whisper your love in my ear and I'm yours forever and more

Your words leave me speechless and that is hard to do

I look at you with wonder, and so grateful that you are you

So my love shine your light upon me, as I will shine for you

Like a lighthouse shines a path for us each to follow

To watch the dawn each day and know we stand together

Our love is strong and keeps getting stronger

To hold your hand in mine and feel the touch of your fingers

As they entwine knowing that I am yours and you are mine forever

You're the sunshine that fades all the darkness in my life.

I've never loved somebody so deeply as you.

I love you greater than I can say. Nothing can ever change my love
for you

When I first noticed you, I was attracted

By your lovely face and your charming smile,

But it was the beauty of your heart that I fell for.

I found an angel in you that's extra wonderful

Than what's seen from outside.

I wake with your love in my thoughts
I feel your love in my body as warm soft caresses
I hear your love whisper and dance in my ears
Am I still dreaming?
Is this real?
Yes my love for you is real and I can feel every thought
As it shows in my body
How I move with the sensuality of my femininity
As I respond to you
The confidence that love brings deep within
The laughter in my eyes as happiness dances in and out of my soul
The beauty I see in you
The strength and compassion
As I rest my head on your heart

I wish the world could hear the song in my head

The music that plays with each breath I take

As I reach for you my love and share this song with you

Filled with love, kindness, compassion and my heart that is true

The way your skin feels under my fingertips

The shiver that runs along my spine

You are the one that holds my heart with your hand in mine

Anything is possible when we put our heads together

You are my king my protector

You hold me safe within your arms so I can rest and love you

I am your queen, I stand by your side and guard your heart

So you can shine

Together we can achieve anything we put our hearts and minds to

A force to be reckoned with

A love so tender, I am happy you are mine.

Every step we take we take together
Every breath is a delight
There is beauty all around us with laughter in our eyes
When I look at you and you are smiling
I can see it in your eyes
You need to do this more often my love as it lights up your face
I see the love you have within and I am so grateful
You chose to share it with me
Smile with your eyes more often my love as I can't help but
smile too
I melt with a giddiness I've never felt before
And just want to see you smile more
To hear you laugh is music to my ears
So much I want to dance
Come grab my hand and dance with me
With laughter in your eyes
And every breath a delight
Through days and years
And the rest of our lives

Every sunrise and sunset look so beautiful

Reflected in your eyes

When the moon rises, and her mystical glow covers the land

Our steps shine like silver in the moonlight

Each step taken together

Each step in time

Our love grows and deepens

Every day and night is a blessing

To be cherished by you as I stand by your side

I am the protector of your heart

As our hearts beat for each other

I feel your heartbeat next to mine

No matter where you are

Distances mean nothing when I can feel your heart in mine

Together as our hearts beat in time

A song is sung with perfect harmony

That reverberates through our souls

Can you feel it love,

Close your eyes

Feel your heartbeat next to mine

Feel my hand in yours

As our lips meet with a gentle caress

That sends my heart into overtime

The look in your eyes shines in mine

As glistening sparkles across space and time

I am there for you my love as you are there for me

Your strength and courage hold me close

As my softness and fierceness hold you dear

Can you feel your heart my love

As he beats in time with me

The song that is sung

As our souls dance together

As our bodies meet and entwine

There is no greater gift I can give you
Except for my love true and pure
It comes from deep within my heart
As she opens wide, it has taken a lifetime to trust
And allow a very special person to step inside
That person, my love, is you
I never thought in this lifetime I would find the one
Who shook me to my core, that made me
Fall in love with myself first so I could fall in love with you
You shake me daily my love
With your words and love for me
Which I never thought I would ever experience.
Some days the doubt creeps in
And then I see your smiling eyes as they look into mine
And the doubt fades away
With each step we take together our love grows and grows
Like a garden filled with flowers of all shades and hues
These colours dance through our souls and colour every step
And show the world the love we have for each other

Honour the call of my heart

Is honouring my soul

As she draws me nearer to you

To embrace love and life

To take that step into the unknown

Of a deep, soulful connection

To deeply know you are desired and loved

With all of my being

This brings a sense of vulnerability my love

I feel it too

Walk this path of love with me so we can grow

My heart leaps knowing that we are and will be together

To truly see you, to be loved heard and seen

So listen to your heart my love, as mine calls out for you

I want to hold your face in my hands

And look deeply into your eyes

The comfort and love I seek is shining brightly within

Hold my hand my love

Pull me close and hold me tight

For your warmth and strength are needed

To soothe my heart and soul

Protect me my love, both my heart and soul

So I never need to fear

Hold me my love and never let go

I am yours and you are mine.

Calm my heart my love as you whisper in my ear

Of all the ways you love me so

To hear, breathe and taste your love

This makes me whole

To feel how you protect me with your words and touch,

I listen carefully as your words are music to my ears

They caress the pain away

Hold me tight my love as I want you by my side

Let me rest with you my love so I may feel safe within your arms

I hear your heartbeat as he keeps in time with mine

I am at peace now my love, safe and happy within your arms.

The gentle touch as your hand brushes over mine
The caress of your skin sends tingles throughout my body
As I brush your hair from your eyes
I see them sparkling with laughter
The pure joy I see bring happiness to my eyes
To share with you the little things
The tender touches
The words whispered to each other
Heads bent forward, touching
Soul nourishing
Heart-warming in the dark before dawn
When we speak of each other
Our grins can't hide
Our faces light up and our whole being shines.

A lazy day in a summer's breeze as you lay your head in my lap
The shadows of the leaves above dance across your skin
As I trace these patterns of the twinkling light across your skin
The laughter in your eyes
And the smile on your lips
I can't help but lean forward and kiss your gorgeous lips
To see you at ease my love, brings my heart so much joy
I can't wait till the day we can spend together an afternoon in the
summer breeze,
And catch the falling leaves of fall
With winter's first snow, your eyes meet mine and you hold me
tight
Walk with me beneath the blossoms of spring with your hand in
mine.
The best thing to hold onto in our life is each other

I remember the days where I felt listened to and understood

When you had my back

When you promised to treat me right

When I was your queen

You said all the right things and found a special place in my heart

That I'm not willing to let you go

I asked for honesty and truth

I thought you did

I now no longer trust myself to know what is right

I remember

I don't want to forget

The feelings I never had before

The way you make me feel

I remember

Where your words and feelings a lie

Or did you truly mean them

About the Author

Louise Kerwin has always been interested in how the body, mind and spirit weave their magic and she has been on a lifelong journey of self-discovery that continues to this day. Louise is a practicing naturopath, kinesiologist, and RAW energies practitioner. She is a soft tissue bodyworker using energy medicine to help her clients move beyond their current limitations. In the last year has delved more deeply into her own inner healing of her heart, which is where this collection of poems has blossomed from.

Born in Christchurch, NZ, Louise now lives in Rockhampton Queensland. ; She has 4 beautiful adult children and 3 grandchildren and two elderly cats as part of her clan.

louisekerwinnaturopath
louise.kerwin
discoverthepoweroftouch.com